Original title:

Bloomy Curves Under the Unicorn Hub

Copyright © 2025 Swan Charm

All rights reserved.

Author: Johan Kirsipuu

ISBN HARDBACK: 978-1-80562-594-0

ISBN PAPERBACK: 978-1-80564-115-5

ISBN HARDBACK: 978-1-80562-594-0
ISBN PAPERBACK: 978-1-80564-115-5

The Celestial Garden's Embrace

In twilight's glow, the petals twirl,
A dance of dreams in a silver whirl.
Stars peek down with a gentle grace,
As whispers linger in the garden's space.

With every breeze, the secrets sigh,
A tapestry woven, low and high.
Moonbeams paint the tender leaves,
Where magic stirs and the heart believes.

From roots that grasp the ancient earth,
To blooms that sing of love and mirth.
Each blossom holds a tale of old,
In colors bright, and stories bold.

The faeries flit on gossamer wings,
While nightingale sweetly softly sings.
In shadows deep, the wishes grow,
In the garden's heart, all secrets flow.

As dawn approaches, the magic swells,
The deep sweet scent of elusive spells.
Each dew-kissed morn, a fresh embrace,
In the celestial garden's quiet place.

Graced by Flora's Whims

In the glade where whispers dwell,
Petals dance like chiming bells.
A bloom of secrets, soft and bright,
Beneath the gaze of moonlit night.

With gentle hands, the breezes weave,
A tapestry that none perceive.
Among the roots, old stories sigh,
Of flowers that to dreams comply.

The Twists of Enchanted Buds

In corners shallow, shadows creep,
Where budding wonders softly sleep.
Twists and turns of nature's grace,
Draw forth the magic, time's embrace.

A fleeting glance, a fleeting chance,
Brings forth the heart in subtle dance.
The blooms emerge, their colors bold,
In whispered tales of ages old.

Gentle Undulations of Nature's Palette

Across the hills, the colors blend,
A soft caress that seems to mend.
The waves of grass, a verdant sea,
Invite the wanderers to be free.

In every stroke, a secret found,
Where echoes of the past abound.
Those gentle slopes, in sunlight's caress,
Cradle the heart in quietness.

Veils of Color in Mythical Landscapes

In lands where myths and dreams converge,
Veils of color begin to surge.
Mountains rise in hues of fire,
Breeding hope, igniting desire.

From valleys deep to skies above,
These shades weave tales of endless love.
Each petal, leaf, and whispered breeze,
A testament to nature's keys.

Dreaming in Petal Shades

In gardens where the whispers play,
Petals flutter soft and gay,
Beneath the moon's enchanting glow,
Dreams bring secrets we shall know.

Each color holds a tale to weave,
In twilight's arms, we shall believe,
With every breath, the night unfolds,
A story wrapped in silken folds.

Upon the breeze, sweet scents arise,
Carried gently to the skies,
Delighting senses, heart's embrace,
In the stillness, find your place.

When morning breaks, the dew will gleam,
Awakening the silent dream,
A symphony of nature's grace,
Awaits the warmth of sun's embrace.

Enigma of the Blooming Veil

Behind the petals, secrets hide,
In colors vibrant, dreams abide,
A veil of bloom, a mystic dance,
Inviting us to take a chance.

Beneath the surface, stories flow,
Whispers of the winds that blow,
A tapestry of night and day,
In floral realms, the lost will stay.

With every step, we draw near,
To timeless echoes we hold dear,
Enigmas wrapped in fragrant grace,
A garden forged from time and space.

The blossoms share their wisdom keen,
In twilight's glow, all feels serene,
For those who seek, a path will show,
In the garden's heart, secrets grow.

Luminescence Among Blooming Shadows

In shadows cast by twilight's hand,
A glow emerges, soft and grand,
Among the blooms that gently sway,
Whispers of light weave night and day.

Petals shimmer, hues divine,
A dance of color, a sacred line,
Each heartbeat echoes Nature's song,
In the twilight where dreams belong.

Through the maze where shadows play,
Lies a path where spirits stay,
With each step, the light reveals,
The beauty in what time conceals.

Among the petals, secrets blend,
In every bud, a tale they send,
Illuminated by the stars,
In the quiet night, lose your scars.

Curved Petal Secrets in Twilight

Curved petals hold a day's refrain,
In twilight whispers, calm and plain,
With every curve, a glimpse of grace,
In nature's arms, a sweet embrace.

The colors blend as day departs,
Composing melodies in hearts,
Secrets dance like fireflies bright,
Illuminating the velvet night.

In silence deep, the stories grow,
From seeds of hope that softly sow,
Each curve a promise, softly spoken,
In the garden, dreams unbroken.

As shadows stretch, the petals sigh,
In the cooling night, beneath the sky,
Curved petal sorrows fade away,
While in their shade, we dare to stay.

Luminescence Among Blooming Shadows

In shadows cast by twilight's hand,
A glow emerges, soft and grand,
Among the blooms that gently sway,
Whispers of light weave night and day.

Petals shimmer, hues divine,
A dance of color, a sacred line,
Each heartbeat echoes Nature's song,
In the twilight where dreams belong.

Through the maze where shadows play,
Lies a path where spirits stay,
With each step, the light reveals,
The beauty in what time conceals.

Among the petals, secrets blend,
In every bud, a tale they send,
Illuminated by the stars,
In the quiet night, lose your scars.

Curved Petal Secrets in Twilight

Curved petals hold a day's refrain,
In twilight whispers, calm and plain,
With every curve, a glimpse of grace,
In nature's arms, a sweet embrace.

The colors blend as day departs,
Composing melodies in hearts,
Secrets dance like fireflies bright,
Illuminating the velvet night.

In silence deep, the stories grow,
From seeds of hope that softly sow,
Each curve a promise, softly spoken,
In the garden, dreams unbroken.

As shadows stretch, the petals sigh,
In the cooling night, beneath the sky,
Curved petal sorrows fade away,
While in their shade, we dare to stay.

Elegies of the Spiraled Petal

In twilight's whisper, petals sigh,
Moonlit secrets caught nearby.
With each bend, a tale unfolds,
In fleeting beauty, life beholds.

Beneath the stars, the dreams reside,
In fragrant gardens, hearts confide.
A tapestry of moments rare,
In spiraled forms, we find our care.

The winds may call, the shadows play,
But in the stillness, echoes stay.
A dance of time, a silent cheer,
In every petal, we draw near.

Softly drifting, the night descends,
Where every memory transcends.
A gentle grace, a love unspoken,
In beauty's hand, no heart is broken.

Tapestry of Colors in a Dreamscape

In fields where colors bleed and blend,
A dreamscape blooms, as heavens send.
Each hue a memory, vivid and bright,
In twilight's arms, we find our light.

The sun's soft glow, a painter's brush,
In every whisper, dreams do rush.
A wonderland where wishes fly,
In every moment, the spirits sigh.

Glimmers of gold and azure waves,
In laughter's echo, the heart enslaves.
As shadows weave with daylight's grace,
In every color, we find our place.

Every petal tells a story old,
In woven threads, the magic's bold.
A tapestry spun from heart and mind,
In dreamscapes, our futures intertwined.

Mystical Curves of Ethereal Flora

In the garden of whispers, curves entwine,
Ethereal blooms in the dusk align.
Each petal sways with secrets deep,
In the moon's embrace, they softly weep.

Faces of nature, soft and strong,
In curves of beauty, where we belong.
A language written in shades of green,
In every blossom, the unseen.

Beneath the gaze of twinkling stars,
Life's delicate dance, no hidden scars.
The silence speaks in fragrant tones,
In mystical curves, love's heart atones.

Where shadows fold and light does play,
In nature's arms, we lose our way.
Ethereal whispers guide the heart,
In every curve, a brand new start.

Fractal Fables of Floral Whispers

In gardens where the fractals spin,
Floral whispers echo within.
Tales of wonder in petals spun,
In nature's breath, life's stories run.

A dance of shapes, the colors bloom,
In fragrant tales, we shed our gloom.
Each whisper weaves through time and space,
In fractal fables, we find our place.

In harmony of shadows cast,
The whispers carry futures vast.
A melody of hearts entwined,
In floral phrases, love defined.

As breezes call, and night draws near,
The tales of petals remain clear.
In fractal forms, our dreams reside,
In whispered fables, we dream wide.

Lush Swirls of Celestial Wonder

In twilight's hush, the stars align,
Their whispers weave a tale divine.
Each twinkle holds a secret bright,
In cosmic dance, they share their light.

The moonbeams brush the earth below,
A silver quilt where fairies glow.
With every breeze, a magic stirs,
Awakening dreams, as night blurs.

In velvet skies, the wishes soar,
Across the realms we can't ignore.
With every sigh, the heavens bloom,
In swirling hues, they chase the gloom.

Nebulas paint the night so vast,
Their colors blend in shadows cast.
A galaxy sings, with heart and grace,
Painting the night with an endless embrace.

So let your thoughts take flight, my dear,
Within this wonder, lose all fear.
For in the celestial winds we find,
The whispers of the boundless mind.

Reveries of a Rainbowed Wonderland

In meadows kissed by sunlit dew,
A canvas stretched in hues so true.
Where blossoms dance, a vivid show,
And every petal sparks a glow.

The rivers sing in colors bright,
Reflecting dreams in morning light.
With laughter shared and love embraced,
In this wonderland, time is chased.

As rain clouds burst in playful spray,
A bow of colors finds its way.
To arch above the fields so green,
A promise kept, a sight serene.

In whispers soft, the breezes play,
As nature hums its wild ballet.
Each creature joins the grand parade,
In harmony, all fears fade.

So close your eyes and wander wide,
Through rainbow paths where dreams abide.
In every corner, joy is found,
In this wonderland, we are unbound.

Twisting Paths through the Narnia of Dreams

In lantern light, the shadows dance,
A world unfolds with a mere glance.
With whispered tales of olden times,
Awakening with gentle chimes.

Through twisting paths of whispered lore,
Each step reveals an open door.
Where fae and giants hold their court,
In hidden glades where dreams consort.

With snowflakes twirling, soft and white,
Beneath the stars, the sky ignites.
From thicket dark to mountain high,
In every breath, the magic lies.

So venture forth, where wonders gleam,
The golden threads of every dream.
For in this realm where shadows play,
The heart will guide you on your way.

So let the moon your compass be,
In dreams, we find our destiny.
With every heartbeat, let love beam,
Through twisting paths, the world will dream.

Harmonious Echoes of Nature's Lullaby

In forest deep, a soft refrain,
The rustle of the leaves, a gain.
A lullaby of nature sings,
As twilight spreads its gentle wings.

The crickets chirp in harmony,
A song of peace, a symphony.
With every note, the soul takes flight,
In evening's grace, the world feels right.

The river's flow is soothing balm,
A whispered rush, a fragrant calm.
Where nightingales serenade the moon,
Their melodies are sweet as tunes.

Each breeze that stirs the fragrant pine,
Caresses dreams, both yours and mine.
In every corner, life aligns,
With nature's heart, our spirit shines.

So listen close, as shadows wane,
To echoes soft, where joy remains.
For in this lullaby, we find,
The threads of peace that you unwind.

Pathways of Petals and Dreams

In the garden where whispers weave,
Through petals soft, and dreams conceive,
Beneath the arch of ancient trees,
Magic dances with the breeze.

Footsteps light on paths of green,
In every shade, a story seen,
The air is thick with fragrant spells,
Each moment lingers, time compels.

Butterflies trace the ties of fate,
In vibrant hues, they celebrate,
A world where laughter reigns supreme,
Awash in warmth, as sunbeams gleam.

Stars descend on velvet nights,
Casting dreams in silver lights,
With every breath, the air imbues,
The magic that the heart pursues.

So tread the trails where blossoms bloom,
Unlock the secrets, venture soon,
For in each petal, a wish resides,
In pathways where the dreamer glides.

Ethereal Currents of Blooms

In the hush of dawn's embrace,
Ethereal currents start to trace,
Flowers wake with tender grace,
Gentle beauty, nature's face.

Whispers float on morning's air,
Where petals blossom, free of care,
Colors brush the canvas bright,
Living art, a pure delight.

Rivers of scent drift and flow,
Carried softly, in breezes low,
Each bloom a tale, a fragrant song,
In the heart where dreams belong.

Moonlit petals shimmer and sway,
As twilight leads the world astray,
In magic's arms, the night draws near,
Embracing all, enchanting here.

So let the currents guide your mind,
In blooms, the treasures you shall find,
A world of wonder waits to greet,
Nature's rhythm—ever sweet.

Glimpses of Fantastical Vegetation

In curious realms where wonders grow,
Glimpses spark, in twilight's glow,
With vines that twist in playful dance,
And flowers weave in bright romance.

Mushrooms glow with inner light,
Guardians of the velvet night,
With secrets whispered to the breeze,
Tales of magic, heart's unease.

Leaves flutter like enchanted wings,
As nature hums, and softly sings,
A tapestry of greens and gold,
A story vast, waiting to unfold.

In this great expanse, behold the grace,
Of fantastical forms, a wondrous place,
Where every petal holds a dream,
And every stem a silken seam.

So wander forth with open eyes,
Amongst the blooms that reach the skies,
Each glimpse a gift, a fleeting spark,
In the world's embrace, no longer dark.

Cascading Petals Beneath Starlight

Underneath the starlit dome,
Cascading petals find their home,
Softly falling, pure and light,
Embracing dreams that fill the night.

Luna's glow upon the stream,
Whispers secrets, woven dreams,
Each blossom kissed by midnight air,
Awakening hopes laid bare.

A carpet laid of colors bright,
Flutters gently in the night,
Nature's gifts, in stillness placed,
In shadows deep, the heart is chased.

As crickets sing their lullabies,
And fireflies dance 'neath velvet skies,
The world unfolds in quiet grace,
In beauty's arms, we lose our place.

So let the petals take you far,
Guided by the evening star,
In cascades of bliss, here you'll find,
The tethering threads of heart and mind.

Spectral Paths of the Mythical

In moonlit woods where shadows weave,
A whisper calls, cannot deceive.
With echoes soft of ancient lore,
The spectral paths unveil once more.

Beneath the arch of twisted trees,
The air is thick with secret pleas.
They speak of worlds both lost and found,
Where myth and magic weave around.

Each footfall stirs the glimmering night,
As wandering souls take graceful flight.
In twilight's grace, the fables gleam,
To dance within a daring dream.

Through misty veils of silver air,
The wistful past begins to stir.
Unfolding tales of star-born light,
Where wonder paints the silent night.

So tread with care upon these trails,
For magic lingers, love prevails.
In spectral paths, the heart does roam,
To find in dreams, a lasting home.

Velvet Curvature of Nature's Art

Beneath the quilt of twilight's fold,
The whispers of the earth unfold.
In every curve, a story sings,
Of hidden paths and wondrous things.

The velvet hue of evening's grace,
Embraces life in softest lace.
Each petal sways, each leaf does sway,
In nature's dance, a grand display.

With fragrant blooms and sunsets bright,
The world awakens to the night.
In every breath, a soft refrain,
A lullaby of joy and pain.

So wander forth in forest deep,
Where secrets of the wild ones sleep.
In nature's arms, feel every beat,
As time drifts on with love's retreat.

Let every moment feel profound,
In velvet curves where dreams are found.
A masterpiece of pure delight,
To hold within the arms of night.

Secrets in the Garden of Dreams

In gardens where the wild things grow,
The secrets hide in ebb and flow.
With petals soft, the stories bloom,
In whispered winds, dispelling gloom.

A lantern glows in twilight's hand,
Illuminating dreams unplanned.
Each shadow dances, grace anew,
In twilight's embrace, the heart breaks through.

The blossoms know, the leaves can tell,
Of every wish cast in the well.
Their colors speak in vibrant sighs,
Of love, of hope, beneath the skies.

With every step within this space,
The world transforms, a gentle race.
In each small heart, a secret gleams,
Untold adventures swirl as dreams.

So linger here, where magic thrums,
In gardens filled with thumping drums.
The secrets swirl in fragrant air,
A tapestry beyond compare.

Spirals of Stardust and Petals

In twilight's fold where stardust swirls,
The magic blooms in spiral twirls.
Each petal glimmers, softly bright,
Painting the canvas of the night.

With every breath, the cosmos sings,
A serenade of hidden things.
In roundabout of dreams' embrace,
The universe unfolds with grace.

It tumbles forth in fragrant streams,
Where hope and wonder weave their themes.
The velvet sky, a canvas wide,
Holds whispers of the souls inside.

Through spirals spun of soft delight,
The heart takes flight, a fearless kite.
In every twinkle, every gleam,
The stars conspire to weave a dream.

So let the petals twirl and sway,
In cosmic dance where shadows play.
In stardust's glow, forever free,
Embrace the magic, just to be.

Celestial Blooms in a Unicorn's Realm

In fields where starlight spills,
Unicorns dance on silver hills.
Blooms with colors bright and bold,
Whisper secrets no one's told.

Through misty paths where wonders play,
Magical creatures glide and sway.
Petal-soft voices fill the air,
With dreams that sparkle everywhere.

Glimmers of dew on emerald blades,
In this realm, where sunlight fades.
Nature's canvas, spun with grace,
Each flower, a tale in space.

Crimson roses, sapphire hues,
Every blossom a spell to choose.
In twilight's arms, they twine and weave,
Creating dreams in hearts that believe.

So linger here, in realms divine,
Where love and magic intertwine.
With every bloom, a silent song,
In unicorn's embrace, we belong.

The Garden Where Wishes Blossom

In a hidden glen, wishes grow,
Bursts of laughter, twinkling glow.
Delicate petals start to sway,
As hope awakens at break of day.

With whispered dreams on fragrant air,
Each blossom tells a tale to share.
Clouds of lavender swirl and spin,
While secret gardens invite us in.

In this sanctuary, time stands still,
Nurtured by magic, love, and will.
Sunlight dances, shadows play,
As wishes bloom in bright array.

Daisies gleam with youthful cheer,
While moonflowers whisper secrets clear.
Every color, a joyful note,
In this garden, wishes float.

So make a wish upon the breeze,
Let the flowers grant you ease.
For in this place where wonders start,
A garden lives inside your heart.

Curvilinear Fantasies of Spring

Beneath a sky of endless blue,
Curves of life and love ring true.
Spring unfurls in soft delight,
Painting dreams in colors bright.

The dance of blossoms, round and free,
Spirals of joy in harmony.
Whispers of laughter fill the air,
As nature sings without a care.

Tender saplings stretch with grace,
Curves and lines in the embrace.
Every petal drips with fate,
In this symphony, we create.

Daylight lingers, shadows play,
As springtime twirls in sweet ballet.
Underneath the golden beams,
We weave our hopes into our dreams.

So let the curves of life be bold,
With stories yet to be told.
In the heart of Spring's sweet song,
We find where we truly belong.

Enchanted Flora in Celestial Embrace

In twilight's glow, enchantments bloom,
Flora dances, dispelling gloom.
Stars twinkle in a velvet sky,
While petals whisper a gentle sigh.

In gardens kissed by lunar light,
Mystic flowers awaken the night.
Veils of mist like dreams transcend,
With every breath, new worlds blend.

Sapphire vines and emerald leaves,
In this haven, the heart believes.
Verse of nature, endlessly twined,
In celestial arms, all is aligned.

Fruited branches sway so slow,
Cradling secrets only they know.
In harmony, the nightingale sings,
Life unfurls on magical wings.

So in these blooms of soft embrace,
Find solace in their gentle grace.
For in the heart of night's soft air,
Enchanted flora dwells everywhere.

Whispers of Enchanted Blossoms

In twilight's glow, the petals gleam,
Soft secrets shared in a silken dream.
Breezes carry tales of old,
In colors vibrant, in whispers bold.

A garden where the fairies play,
In shadows deep, where night holds sway.
With each rustle, a story flows,
Of magic's touch, where wonder grows.

Among the blooms, a gentle sigh,
As starlit wishes drift and fly.
In fragrant whispers, softly spun,
Life's sweet tapestry now begun.

The moonlight bathes the petals bright,
In silver threads of shimmering light.
Where dreams are woven, hearts entwined,
In enchanted realms, forever kind.

So linger here, in twilight's grace,
Where nature unfolds its warm embrace.
A symphony in bloom's soft song,
In whispered magic, we belong.

Serpentine Petals of Fantasy

In a twilight garden, shadows creep,
Serpentine petals in silence weep.
Each curve and twist a tale they weave,
Of dreams believed and hearts that grieve.

Beneath the stars, where magic stirs,
A dance of colors, a flurry of furs.
Soft melodies on the evening air,
As enchanting whispers thread with care.

Among the thorns of vibrant hues,
Hidden treasures await the few.
Each blossom a secret, a message imbued,
In the tapestry of fate, we're pursued.

With every sigh of the cool night breeze,
Ancient stories wrap 'round the trees.
In this realm of mystical sights,
The world transforms on moonlit nights.

So tread with wonder, let your heart soar,
Embrace the magic, crave for more.
For in this garden, dreams can bind,
Serpentine petals where hearts unwind.

The Arcane Garden's Dance

Amid the twilight, shadows blend,
In the arcane garden, magic does mend.
Petals a-twirl in a vibrant trance,
Nature's charm leads the dance.

With ancient whispers woven tight,
In the soft glow of starlit night.
Each bloom a spirit, each leaf a song,
In the garden's embrace, we belong.

Figures glide on the moon-kissed path,
As laughter echoes in nature's bath.
Where flora rises, a symphony plays,
In beats of magic, lost in a daze.

So let your soul take flight with ease,
In enchanting breezes, find your peace.
With every step, let wonder flow,
In the arcane garden, time stands slow.

Together we twirl in a blissful spin,
In this hidden realm, let love begin.
In petals and dreams, we find our way,
In the garden's heart, forever stay.

Ethereal Blossoms in Moonlight

Beneath the canopy of the night,
Ethereal blossoms bathe in light.
Soft hues awaken, shimmering bright,
In the embrace of celestial sight.

With whispers carried on dewy air,
Dreams dance lightly, free of care.
Where shadows weave with beams of gold,
Ancient magic in stillness unfolds.

Each petal whispers a tale untold,
In moonlit gardens, bold yet cold.
As twilight lingers, a spell ensnares,
In blooming wonders, no one dares.

A gentle breeze stirs the night's song,
Calling forth spirits, where we belong.
In the serenade of a soft embrace,
Ethereal wonders, time leaves no trace.

So let your heart be open wide,
To the dance of the blossoms where dreams abide.
In moonlight's glow, let spirits soar,
Ethereal beauty forevermore.

Celestial Petals in a Whirlwind

In twilight's glow, the petals soar,
Dancing softly, forever more.
Whispers of stars in a gentle sway,
Carried on winds, they drift away.

Through skies of azure, they twist and twine,
A ballet of colors, bright and divine.
Moonbeams catch their soft embrace,
Every flutter, a fleeting trace.

They brush the heavens, a silken thread,
In the warmth of dreams, where hopes are fed.
With each turn, the world ignites,
In a symphony of twinkling lights.

Softly landing on the earth below,
A reminder of magic, a gentle glow.
With every breeze, they weave their tale,
Celestial whispers on the gale.

Together they dance, a timeless flight,
Through the endless depths of night.
With every petal, a dream unfurls,
In the whirlwind's heart, they spin in swirls.

Dreamscapes of Curved Enchantment

In vivid hues, the dreamers tread,
Paths of wonder, where few have led.
Curved enchantments beckon near,
In this realm, we lose our fear.

Glowing whispers in the hush of night,
Wrap around us, soft and light.
Through enchanting woods, we weave and play,
Chasing shadows that slip away.

Each whispered word like a soft caress,
Pulls us deeper into the blessed.
In the gentle arms of fantasy's reign,
We find our solace, escape the pain.

Gold-tipped flowers bloom and sway,
In melodies where wishes lay.
As time drifts by, we come alive,
In dreamscapes where our spirits thrive.

We gather starlight in our hands,
As laughter echoes through the lands.
In this realm of magic spun,
Every heart beats as one.

The Floral Archways of Infinity

Beneath the archways, blossoms bloom,
Painting pathways that chase the gloom.
Their vibrant colors stretch the skies,
In every petal, a thousand sighs.

They whisper secrets of ages past,
In fragrant tales that forever last.
As we wander through the winding lanes,
A world of wonder in sweet refrains.

Beneath the canopies of hues so bright,
We lose ourselves in sheer delight.
Every turn, a new surprise,
In the floral embrace, magic lies.

With every brush of the cool, soft air,
We dance unchained, without a care.
In this realm, time slips away,
Leaving only joy where shadows play.

As dusk descends and petals close,
A gentle promise, the heart bestows.
In the archways of dreams, we find our way,
In the dance of colors, forever stay.

Spirals of Color and Light

A spiral of dreams, like a vibrant kite,
Soaring upward into the night.
Colors blend and swirl so free,
In the cosmos, we long to be.

With every turn, a new delight,
Painting the darkness, igniting the light.
From crimson red to ocean blue,
In this tapestry, our spirits flew.

Each flash of brilliance, a gleaming spark,
Guiding us through the deep and dark.
In every hue, a story to share,
In the spirals of magic, we're bound to dare.

Together we twirl in this wondrous flight,
Hands intertwined, hearts alight.
Through the whirling galaxies, we race,
Living in the rhythm, a cosmic embrace.

In the end, when colors all blend,
A circle of life that will not end.
In the spiral's heart, we find our peace,
In a world where love will never cease.

Enchanted Spirals of the Divine Garden

In the garden's heart, whispers sing,
Petals twirl like an elegant ring,
Colors blend in a tender embrace,
Life emerges in this sacred space.

Beneath the arch of an ancient tree,
Secrets dance, wild and free,
A melody hums through the leaves,
As the evening light gently weaves.

Fountains glisten with silvered grace,
Reflecting joy in every trace,
And shadows play on the soft, cool ground,
In this haven, enchantment is found.

With every step, the magic stirs,
Awakening dreams and sweet murmurs,
The spirals twist, inviting each soul,
To wander deep within the whole.

Among the blooms where the fairies glide,
Secrets of old in the petals hide,
In the enchanted garden's pure light,
The world feels wondrously bright.

A Dance of Vivid Petals

A dance of petals in the breeze,
Twisting and turning with such ease,
With each step, their colors bloom,
Creating splendor that fills the room.

In the sunlit glades where they sway,
Nature's artistry comes out to play,
Every hue a song to share,
As laughter fills the fragrant air.

In the midst of a symphony bright,
Waltzing blossoms twinkle in flight,
They rise and fall to a melody sweet,
Caressing the earth with delightful feet.

Whispers of joy in twinkling light,
Each petal's dance, a pure delight,
Life unfolds with a soft embrace,
Bringing a smile to every face.

As they echo through the lush green lands,
Their charm weaves hopes within our hands,
In this vibrant realm where dreams take root,
They inspire our hearts in a dance so astute.

The Symphony of Nature's Curved Palette

Awake to the symphony's gentle call,
Where colors arise, and shadows fall,
Nature hums in a heartfelt tone,
Each brushstroke whispers, never alone.

With blooms like notes upon a staff,
They share their tales, making us laugh,
As the breeze carries their sweet refrain,
Painting landscapes of joy and pain.

Curves of the earth weave tales untold,
In vibrant shades of green and gold,
Every wave of grass, each tree so tall,
In this living orchestra, we feel it all.

As sun and moon take turns to play,
The canvas shifts from dusk to day,
Colors swirl in a lively dance,
Inviting all to take a chance.

Through sparkling streams and fragrant fields,
Nature's magic softly yields,
A symphony of life that draws us near,
In every petal, a world so dear.

Shimmering Trails Through Fairy Grounds

Along the paths where fairies tread,
Shimmering trails of silver thread,
Whispers echo through the emerald glades,
As twilight weaves its fleeting shades.

Each step awakes the hidden charm,
In this realm where dreams disarm,
Glimmers dance atop the moss,
Reminding us of love's great gloss.

With laughter rippling through the trees,
A gentle tune upon the breeze,
The twilight beckons, softly calling,
In fairy grounds where magic's sprawling.

Beneath the stars, their visions gleam,
Illuminating our wildest dream,
A world alive with sights so rare,
As we wander without a care.

So follow the trails, let wonder lead,
Through fairy grounds where hearts are freed,
In every sparkle, every spark,
Adventure waits within the dark.

Twilit Paths Wrapped in Magic Mist

On twilit paths where shadows dance,
The mist wraps round in secret chance.
With whispered tales of olden nights,
And stars that twinkle, soft and light.

Each step we take, the shadows sigh,
Beneath the arch of an ancient sky.
The air is thick with stories spun,
Of dreams awakened, joys begun.

Through silvered leaves the breezes blow,
And every turn reveals a glow.
A flicker here, a shimmer there,
In the enchanting evening air.

The moonlight paints a path so bright,
Guiding us gently through the night.
With every breath, the magic swells,
As if the world has cast its spells.

So let us wander, hand in hand,
Through this delightful, fairy land.
For every twist and turn we face,
Is wrapped in timeless, wondrous grace.

Colors That Whisper Secrets of the Night

In colors deep, secrets abide,
Wrapped in shadows, they confide.
Crimson dreams and sapphire skies,
Each hue a tale, each glance a prize.

Emerald whispers in the breeze,
Awakening thoughts with gentle ease.
Golden threads of moonlit gleam,
Unfolding softly, like a dream.

Indigo nights, where wishes flow,
Painting the landscapes, putting on a show.
A palette rich with life and lore,
Each shade a world to explore.

Silvery stars, like jewels of frost,
Guide us past what we thought was lost.
A kaleidoscope of echoes blend,
In the night, where colors mend.

So let us dance in this dusky glow,
Where colors whisper, and secrets grow.
For in the night, each brush stroke bright,
Courses through hearts, igniting light.

Curved Reflections in a Prism of Joy

In prisms bright, reflections swirl,
Creating joy, a canvas unfurl.
Each light that bends, a moment pure,
An echo of laughter we all can share.

Curved reflections, soft and warm,
In every heart, they weave their charm.
A dappled sunlit path we tread,
With vibrant dreams that dance ahead.

As hues collide, we find our way,
In the spectrum of a brand new day.
With open arms, we greet the shine,
Reveling in the joy divine.

Through playful colors, life ignites,
In swirling laughter, pure delights.
Each memory made, a brushstroke true,
On the canvas of me and you.

So let us twirl in this resplendent light,
Where joy is born and hearts take flight.
In every curve, a story unfolds,
In layers of love, our lives are told.

Veils of Wonder in the Heart of Enchantment

Beyond the veil, a world awaits,
Where wonder stirs and magic creates.
In every glimmer, in every spark,
Lies a tale waiting to embark.

Whispers of old through gardens weave,
In hopes and dreams we dare to believe.
With enchanted steps, we venture forth,
To seek the treasures of the mirth.

The heart of night sings soft and low,
Of hidden realms where spirits glow.
Veils of mystery, tucked away,
Guarding secrets from the day.

In moonlit glades, enchantment waits,
With every turn, the heart elates.
Through veils of wonder, we shall find,
The magic that unites our minds.

So let us wander, hand in hand,
Through this bewitched and wondrous land.
For in the heart, where dreams take flight,
Lies the essence of pure delight.

Fantastical Blooming Tides

In secret glades where shadows play,
The flowers dance in bright array.
With whispers soft like evening's breath,
They tell their tales of life and death.

The tides of time in colors swirl,
As petals drift and dreams unfurl.
In twilight's glow, the magic weaves,
A symphony that never leaves.

Each blossom holds a wish within,
A universe where hopes begin.
With every breeze, the stories blend,
A tapestry with no clear end.

Beneath the moon, the dreams take flight,
In gardens kissed by silver light.
The earth and sky together sigh,
As wondrous nights begin to fly.

So wander through this hazy spell,
And find the secrets flowers tell.
For in their hearts, the magic lies,
A treasure seen through dreaming eyes.

Petal Dreams Beneath the Stars

Beneath the stars, where wishes gleam,
The world is wrapped in a gentle dream.
With petals soft as whispered sighs,
They dance like echoes in twilight skies.

Moonlight drapes the gardens fair,
Where every breath holds fragrant air.
Each bloom a spell, each hue a rhyme,
In night's embrace, we trace through time.

The silver paths of starlit gleams,
Guide hearts that wander into dreams.
In shadows deep, the secrets bloom,
While night unfolds its velvet room.

The petals flutter on the breeze,
A symphony that brings sweet ease.
Time pauses in this sacred space,
Where all can find their rightful place.

So linger longer, let hopes soar,
In gardens lost, you'll find much more.
For every petal has a tale,
A story spun in magic's veil.

Hidden Petals of Celestial Tales

In worlds unseen, the petals hide,
Whispers of time and skies collide.
With laughter light like summer's breeze,
They weave together ancient trees.

Each blossom holds a secret song,
A melody that draws us strong.
In twilight's hush, the stories swell,
A magic spun where shadows dwell.

The stars above, like jewels bright,
Illuminate the quiet night.
With every bloom, a wish takes flight,
As hearts unite in pure delight.

Beneath the sky, the tales entwine,
In gardens where the sun will shine.
A tapestry of dreams will grow,
With hidden paths for souls to know.

So take a step where petals lie,
And chase the echoes through the sky.
For every hidden bud conveys,
The light of life in wondrous ways.

Vibrant Pathways of Colorful Whimsy

Along the paths of vibrant hue,
The flowers whisper secrets true.
With laughter bright and colors bold,
Their stories dance, forever told.

A tapestry of dreams unspooled,
In every garden, magic ruled.
The petals twirl, a joyous sight,
In harmony with day and night.

With every turn, a new delight,
In pathways kissed by morning light.
The world transforms as colors blend,
No boundaries where the heart can mend.

So take a leap into this realm,
Where whimsy guides and dreams overwhelm.
For in this space, you shall always find,
The vibrant threads of heart and mind.

So join the dance, embrace the glee,
In every flower, there's magic free.
With every step, the wonders bloom,
Creating joy that chases gloom.

The Shape of Magic Beneath Silver Light

In shadows deep, where whispers wake,
The silver light starts to quake.
Like flickering stars, the spells unfold,
Magic takes shape, bright and bold.

Through ancient woods, with secrets rife,
It dances softly, full of life.
A waltz of wands, a gentle sway,
Enchanting hearts in twilight's play.

With twinkling eyes, the faeries gleam,
In moonlit realms, they softly dream.
The air is thick with whispered lore,
An echo from the ages yore.

As night descends, the shadows blend,
With every turn, the tales extend.
In stillness found, the magic stirs,
Revealing sight beyond the blurs.

An omen bright, a fleeting glance,
That twirls the heart to join the dance.
A tapestry of fate and light,
The shape of magic, pure delight.

Whimsical Growths of Mystical Origins

In gardens wild, where colors sing,
Emerald sprigs with secrets cling.
Fantastical blooms in shadows lie,
With whispered hopes, they reach and sigh.

Their petals soft, in starlit hues,
Each one a charm, each one a muse.
Sprouted from dreams, they twist and twine,
In delicate patterns, they intertwine.

With laughter light, they paint the air,
In every scent, a hint of care.
A flick of light, a spark of cheer,
In whimsy's grasp, the world feels near.

Beneath the moon, their magic plays,
A vibrant dance through twilight's haze.
They weave enchantments, bold and bright,
In whispers shared with the daring night.

These growths arise from dreams of old,
In gardens where the brave are bold.
Awash in wonder, soft as a sigh,
The whimsical blooms never die.

Petal-Wrapped Dreams in Twilight

In twilight's hush, when day departs,
Dreams unfold in delicate parts.
Wrapped in petals of softest grace,
A gentle kiss upon the face.

They drift through realms of softest night,
Where wishes danced in silver light.
With every breath, a thought takes flight,
As shadows weave the coming light.

Soft whispers spin in fragrant air,
Each layered dream, a heartfelt prayer.
Kissed by stars, their glow ignites,
In quiet moments, magic excites.

They cradle hopes, both small and grand,
In gentle hands, faithful and planned.
With laughter sweet, they pirouette,
In twilight's glow, they'll not forget.

For every petal holds a wish,
The kind that dreams cannot dismiss.
A tapestry of night's embrace,
Petal-wrapped dreams in sacred space.

Phantasy Blooms of Otherworldly Nature

In realms beyond the mortal sight,
Phantasy blooms with pure delight.
Colors merge in a dance so rare,
Crafted visions, light as air.

They sway beneath the cosmic tides,
Where every flower a secret hides.
With sparkling hues of ethereal light,
They draw the gaze, enchanting night.

From stardust born, they weave and spin,
A chance to glimpse what lies within.
The whispers of forgotten days,
In phantasy blooms, the magic plays.

Through portals wide, the journeys call,
Where petals rise, and shadows fall.
In serenades of moonbeam's kiss,
The world's reborn in vibrant bliss.

Beneath the veil of cosmic dreams,
In every hush, reality seems.
For nature's art, in wonder's name,
Phantasy blooms ignite the flame.

Nature's Dance on Spiraled Pathways

Whispers of breeze twirl leaves in delight,
The sun blinks gently, casting golden light.
Beneath the canopies, shadows sway slow,
While creatures awaken, secrets to show.

Moss carpets ground like a soft, green gown,
Each footstep echoes, never a frown.
Birds serenade from branches up high,
While clouds drift softly across the blue sky.

Rivers hum softly as they wend their way,
Dancing with pebbles, in joyful array.
A symphony crafted by nature's great hand,
In this lush, vibrant, ever-changing land.

Wildflowers burst forth in colors so bright,
Painting the earth with strokes of pure light.
The cycle of life, in rhythm, it flows,
In harmony stitched where the wild beauty grows.

As twilight descends, the stars blossom clear,
Their shimmering laughter, a song we hold dear.
Nature's embrace, like a warm, gentle sigh,
Invites weary travelers beneath the vast sky.

Flowering Reveries through Enchanted Grounds

In gardens adorned with emerald dreams,
Petals unfurling like soft silken seams.
The fragrance of dusk mingles with light,
As magic awakens at the end of the night.

Amidst the trellis, vines whisper sweet lines,
Of secrets and stories and ancient designs.
Butterflies flutter, like whispers of grace,
Dancing on blossoms in this sacred space.

Moonlight unveils a pearl-studded cloak,
Where dreams take flight, and starlight can soak.
Each flower a wish, each bloom a tale told,
In the language of petals, soft and bold.

Hushed are the echoes of wandering feet,
For this enchanted realm feels like a heartbeat.
Every turn whispers of wonders anew,
As moments unfold in shades of deep blue.

Through arched pathways, the echoes remain,
In flowered reveries where joy is our gain.
Feel every heartbeat, entwined with the night,
In this lush, precious world, bathed in soft light.

Cascade of Blooms in Surreal Hues

A tapestry woven with fine silver threads,
In the cascade of blooms, where the silence treads.
Iridescent colors that shimmer and sway,
Invite every dreamer to linger and stay.

Lilies like lanterns, glowing so bright,
Reflecting the echoes of fading daylight.
With petals like whispers, they beckon the heart,
To dance in the gardens, where wonders impart.

In the crest of the hills where the wildflowers peek,
Their laughter a language that none dare to speak.
Unfolding horizons where visions take flight,
As day turns to dusk, and then back into night.

From lavender valleys to valleys of gold,
Each bloom a memoir, a story retold.
In surreal hues, they fall softly like rain,
A cascade of dreams, free from worry or pain.

These blossoms of hues weave time into song,
Holding the memories where we all belong.
In nature's vast canvas, so quietly fused,
The heart finds its solace in colors confused.

Radiant Arcs of Mythical Flora

In enchanted arboretums of vibrant delight,
Radiant arcs rise, kissed by soft twilight.
Petals like fabrics, woven in grace,
Entwined with the magic that drapes every space.

Golden evening washes the skies with soft hue,
As fantastical creatures emerge into view.
From thickets and shadows, they twirl and they weave,
In the dance of the flora, they linger, believe.

Ferns unfurl secrets, mysteries concealed,
In the arms of the trees, where beauty is revealed.
With each breath entwined in the scent of sweet earth,
Life sings in the whispers, celebrating rebirth.

Flowers in bloom with their radiant glow,
Unraveling dreams like an intricate show.
In gardens of wonder, each petal reflects,
The stories of magic our heart ever seeks.

As the night draws near, and the stars come to play,
The arcs of the flora dance gently away.
In the glow of the moonlight, they shimmer and sway,
Awakening echoes of magic they lay.

Curves of Magic and Reverie

In shadows dance the flickering light,
Whispers of wonder, embrace the night.
Curves of magic twist through the air,
Reveries linger, as dreams lay bare.

Stars drip laughter, like honeyed dew,
Each spark a wish that ignites anew.
In twilight's canvas, secrets unfold,
The heart finds solace, the spirit bold.

Tender echoes of laughter bloom,
In moments fleeting, dispelling gloom.
A symphony woven of silken threads,
Where courage awakens and magic spreads.

In corners hidden, instincts align,
With drifts of stardust, our spirits entwine.
Curves of magic weave destinies true,
In the fabric of night, where dreams come through.

So dance, dear wanderer, through veils of mirth,
Where love's soft whispers cradle the earth.
In curves of magic, let your heart soar,
For in reverie, we are forever more.

Ethereal Currents in a Dreamscape

A river flows through realms of thought,
Carried by whispers, in silence sought.
Ethereal currents drift and glide,
In the embrace of the dreamer's tide.

Clouds of wonder blanket the night,
Painting horizons in soft twilight.
With each beat, the heart starts to roam,
In this dreamscape, we find our home.

Glistening visions, like dew on grass,
Moments unfurl, as shadows pass.
Within this realm, lost souls take flight,
Mortals awaken, from darkness to light.

Floating on whispers, we chase the stars,
Each glowing ember, a glimpse from afar.
Ethereal currents, gentle and bright,
Guide our spirits through time's endless night.

So linger a while in these mystic streams,
Where reality dances with woven dreams.
In this dreamscape, let your heart sway,
For within the currents, magic shall stay.

Serendipitous Blooms of the Radiant

In gardens lush, a treasure lies,
Serendipitous blooms, 'neath blushing skies.
Petals unfurl with a soft embrace,
Each fragrant whisper brings joy to the space.

Radiant colors beckon the bees,
In gentle harmony with the rustling trees.
Nature's brush dips in sunlit gold,
As stories of magic in silence unfold.

Dreams take root in the fertile earth,
Where laughter dances, and life finds mirth.
With every bloom, a promise takes shape,
In the heart of the garden, wonder escapes.

Glistening raindrops, like diamonds shine,
Kissing each petal, a touch divine.
Serendipitous blooms rise from the ground,
In their beauty, a symphony found.

So wander through paths of fragrant delight,
Let the spirit soar, wrapped in the light.
In these blooms, as the world hums along,
We find our solace, where hearts belong.

The Magical Garden of Surreal Forms

In gardens vast, where dreams conspire,
The magical blooms dance in desire.
Amidst the petals of colors bright,
Surreal forms shimmer under the light.

Each whispered breeze carries tales untold,
Of wonders woven in marigold.
As shadows waltz with the light of day,
The garden beckons, inviting to play.

Beneath the arches of ancient trees,
The air is rich with a fragrant tease.
Here, imagination finds its muse,
In every corner, a vision to choose.

Mirrors reflect the sky's endless hue,
In crystal waters, dreams come true.
The magical garden breathes and sighs,
With every moment, a moment that flies.

So step inside, let the magic begin,
Where surreal forms whisper secrets within.
In this wondrous realm, let the heart roam free,
For the garden awaits, just for you and me.

Trails of Flowering Mirth

In the woods where laughter blooms,
The air is filled with joyous tunes.
Gossamer wings, a fleeting sight,
Dance with shadows in the light.

Where the brook with secrets flows,
Whispers weave through petals' throes.
Each step taken, a melody,
Embraced by nature's harmony.

Flowers bloom in vibrant hues,
Bearing tales of morning dews.
Joyous hearts beneath the sun,
Chasing dreams that had begun.

Twilight paints the skies in gold,
Stories of the young and old.
Stardust mingles in the breeze,
Wrapping all in tranquil ease.

With every bloom the magic grows,
In this place where kindness flows.
Let your laughter be the guide,
In this realm where hearts abide.

Songs of the Enchanted Flora

Deep in glades where wonders weave,
The flowers hum and softly cleave.
Voices rise with softest sigh,
In sweet symphony of the sky.

Petals drift on zephyr's glee,
Singing songs in harmony.
Through the thicket, sounds will ring,
Of the joy that spring will bring.

Roots entwined beneath the earth,
Cradle dreams of endless mirth.
Each blossom holds a tale untold,
In their warmth, the world unfolds.

Once the moon ascends the night,
Stars will twinkle, pure and bright.
Echoes linger; whispers flow,
In the garden's heart, we grow.

Through the seasons, life will thrive,
In this space, we feel alive.
Every flower, thread of fate,
In the magic, we create.

Garden of Whimsy and Grace

In the garden where dreams take flight,
Every corner bursts with light.
Tiny fairies spin and play,
As the world begins to sway.

Winding paths of emerald green,
Glistening under sunbeam's sheen.
Petals whisper secrets shared,
In this haven, none are spared.

Butterflies, like jewels in air,
Twirl and dance without a care.
A symphony of colors bright,
Crafting tales of pure delight.

Clouds drift lazily, soft as cream,
A playful canvas for a dream.
In this garden, hearts take wing,
Unraveled tales our spirits sing.

Every hour here brings a gift,
Nature's charm, the heart will lift.
In laughter's echo, we embrace,
The enchanting, whimsical space.

Kaleidoscope of Celestial Blooms

In a realm where colors blend,
Celestial blooms, our hearts commend.
Brighten pathways with their glow,
Guiding souls to where dreams flow.

Stars descend to kiss the earth,
Giving every flower worth.
Each a prism of delight,
Flashing visions in the night.

Glistening under moonlit skies,
Softly hum their lullabies.
Each petal holds a universe,
In whispers light, they will converse.

Time stands still as night unfolds,
In reflections, love's story told.
With every breath, the magic grows,
In the heart where wonder flows.

In this garden of fleeting grace,
Life discovers its true place.
Through a kaleidoscope's embrace,
We find the beauty we all chase.

The Dance of Petals in the Stardust Air

In the still of night, petals gleam,
Caught in a whisper, they float like a dream.
Beneath the moon's gentle, watchful gaze,
They twirl and twist in a starry haze.

Softly they drift on the cool night breeze,
Awakening magic with elegant ease.
Each petal a story, a world yet untold,
Carried by wishes, so precious, so bold.

With laughter of sprites in the shadows they play,
As echoes of starlight beckon their way.
In spirals and swirls, they dance without care,
An enchanting ballet in the stardust air.

Time curls and bends where enchantments reside,
In gardens of wonder, where secrets abide.
A tapestry woven from twilight's soft thread,
In the still of the night, dreams warmly spread.

So let us join in, let our spirits take flight,
Where petals and stardust invite us tonight.
And together we'll dance, with the world far away,
In the magic of moments where hearts choose to stay.

Surreal Gardens Under Twilight's Embrace

Under twilight's veil, the lanterns ignite,
In surreal gardens, a magical sight.
Petals of sapphire, and emerald leaves,
Whisper secrets only the moon believes.

Winding pathways of mist and delight,
Invite wayward souls to wander by night.
Where shadows of dreams steal glances and sway,
And time slips away like the end of the day.

With colors that dance in a soft, muted hue,
Each moment in twilight is vivid and new.
In the heart of the garden, where wonders unfold,
The stories of stardust in silence are told.

With every step taken on this sacred ground,
The whispers of magic, enchanting, abound.
Embraced by the twilight, we breathe in the air,
And lose all our worries, feel light as a prayer.

Thus linger we shall, as the night stretches wide,
In surreal gardens, with dreams as our guide.
For here in the twilight, where dreams softly soar,
We embrace all the magic forevermore.

Luminous Whirls of Echoed Laughter

In the heart of the night, laughter takes flight,
Luminous whirls dance, painting the night.
With shadows and whispers, they twirl through the air,
Inviting all dreamers to join with a flair.

Like fireflies flickering in spirit and play,
The echoes of joy chase the stillness away.
Each note in the night sings of cheerful delight,
As starlight and laughter create purest light.

With shimmer and spark, every giggle ignites,
The air filled with magic, as wonder invites.
A symphony swirling, both playful and grand,
As echoing laughter brings dreams close at hand.

In the dance of the evening, all troubles depart,
For joy is a journey that flows from the heart.
In the glow of the laughter, our spirits entwine,
We celebrate moments that sparkle and shine.

So come, take my hand, let us dance through the night,
Where luminous whirls make the world feel so bright.
In echoes of laughter, our hearts will be free,
Together we'll wander, forever in glee.

Fragrant Dreams in the Land of Fable

In the land of fable, where dreams take their shape,
Fragrant whispers of magic, in stillness escape.
Each flower a promise, each leaf holds a tale,
In the garden of wonders, where fantasies sail.

With colors that blend in the soft morning light,
Hopes linger gently, like birds in their flight.
The air is a potion, both sweet and profound,
Inviting our hearts to explore the unknown.

In fields where the dreams and the legends unfold,
The fragrance of stories is daring and bold.
Where every petal reveals a new way,
And the land sings of magic that brightens the day.

Let's wander through pathways where wishes take wing,
In the land of fable, where joy makes us sing.
With hope as our compass, we dance with the breeze,
In fragrant dreams woven with laughter and ease.

For here in this haven, where fantasies flow,
The heart finds its rhythm, and spirits will glow.
In the land of fable, where dreams intertwine,
We'll weave timeless tales, forever divine.

Where Fantasies Dance in Technicolor

In realms where colors burst and twirl,
A vibrant dream begins to curl.
Where shadows whisper tales of old,
And mysteries in hues unfold.

With laughter spun in threads of gold,
Each heart a story waiting to be told.
The skies alight with magic's flare,
As fantasies drift on the autumn air.

Beneath a canopy of sparkling night,
The stars awake, a wondrous sight.
They weave a tapestry of desire,
As wishes flicker like a fire.

Through laughter's echo, spirits rise,
As dreams unfold under midnight skies.
In every breath, a chance to sing,
Where hope ignites on enchanted wing.

Spirals of Light in the Fairy Glade

In glades where fairies spin and weave,
The light entwines as shadows leave.
Soft petals dance in gentle breeze,
A tune of magic through the trees.

The air is thick with wonder's spark,
As whispers float through the vibrant dark.
With every flicker, secrets bloom,
As glimmers sweep away all gloom.

A patchwork quilt of dreams laid wide,
Where hope and joy forever abide.
Beneath the arches of emerald fair,
The universe hums a lullaby rare.

As moonlight spills on emerald ground,
In spirals bright, new worlds abound.
Each step a promise, each glance a spell,
Where wishes born in silence swell.

Gardens Blooming with Dreams Untold

In gardens lush where whispers grow,
Soft petals share their tales below.
With colors bright like thoughts unfurled,
They cradle dreams within this world.

Among the blooms, the fairies play,
In light of dawn, they greet the day.
Each blossom holds a secret sweet,
In fragrant paths where wonders meet.

From violets shy to roses bold,
The stories of the heart unfold.
In every shade, in every hue,
A tapestry of wishes new.

The garden hums with life and grace,
As dreams awaken to find their place.
With every rustle, magic swells,
In this domain where beauty dwells.

Whimsical Sways of Moonlit Fantasies

In moonlit nights, the whispers play,
As shadows dance and drift away.
With every flicker of silver light,
The garden blooms with dreams of night.

Where laughter stirs in the cool, sweet air,
And fantasies twine in love's affair.
With each step, the world transforms,
As hearts ignite in joyous storms.

Beneath the stars, the world feels new,
In every glance, a magic view.
The night unveils its gentle grace,
Inviting all who dare embrace.

As shadows weave their playful tune,
The whispers linger, soft as June.
In moonlit charm, we sway and dream,
In whimsical realms where glories gleam.

Mystical Weavings of Petal Varieties

In twilight's breath, the petals glow,
Threads of magic sway and flow.
From deep within the garden's heart,
A tapestry of dreams does start.

Whispers blend in colors bright,
Crafting shadows, soft as night.
Each bloom a secret, rich and rare,
A dance of fragrance fills the air.

In every fold of silken hue,
Stories of old, in morning dew.
With every petal, a tale unfolds,
A realm of wonder, brightly bold.

Beneath the sky, the colors twist,
In nature's hand, nothing missed.
The weavings sing, with silken grace,
Through time and space, they find their place.

A garden path where fairies tread,
Upon the dreams that softly spread.
With every step, a journey new,
In mystical shades, the heart beats true.

Resplendent Blossoms in Dreamt Gardens

In gardens where the shadows play,
Resplendent blooms greet the day.
They whisper secrets to the breeze,
With every sway, they bring us peace.

Among the hues, a laughter bright,
In petals soft as morning light.
They tell of wishes, hopes that soar,
In dreamt gardens, we explore.

Fragrant notes fill the open air,
With every bloom, a tale laid bare.
A symphony of colors bright,
In nature's arms, a pure delight.

Each blossom sings a sweet refrain,
Reminding us of joy and pain.
In every leaf, a story's spun,
A dance of life, where love's begun.

Resplendent whispers, hearts entwined,
In dreamt gardens, peace we find.
A canvas crafted by the skies,
In every petal, magic lies.

Creatures in Lush Horizons

In shadows deep where creatures dwell,
Whispers weave a looping spell.
With gentle steps they roam the night,
In lush horizons, pure delight.

From flowering leaves and grasses sway,
Their playful forms come out to play.
With sparkling eyes and hearts so free,
They dance beneath the silver tree.

The foxes prance, the owls they call,
In harmony, they share it all.
A symphony of rustling leaves,
In nature's arms, the heart believes.

Creatures wise, with stories spun,
Beneath the stars, the night's begun.
Each heartbeat echoes through the glade,
In lush horizons, dreams are laid.

With every dawn and dusk anew,
The creatures weave their stories true.
In every corner, life takes flight,
In lush horizons, pure delight.

Spirals of Lush Vibrations

In spirals soft, the vibrations rise,
A symphony beneath the skies.
Each note, a whisper, sweet and clear,
A call to all who dare to hear.

With every turn, a dance of light,
In vibrant shades, our souls ignite.
The rhythm pulses, heartbeats blend,
In lush vibrations, time does bend.

The blossoms sway, the leaves partake,
In gentle waves, the world will wake.
A cascade of colors, pure and free,
In spirals of joy, we find our key.

Together we sway, lost in the sound,
In lush vibrations, magic found.
With every heartbeat, every sigh,
The spirals lift us to the sky.

So come and dance where nature sings,
In vibrant realms, the spirit clings.
Spirals of life, forever spun,
In lush vibrations, we are one.

Spirited Fronds Beneath Ethereal Vistas

In twilight's grasp, the fronds do sway,
Beneath the stars, where shadows play.
Their whispers weave through night's embrace,
In dreams we float to a wondrous place.

With every breath, the air is spun,
Of stories tall and battles won.
In silver glades, the spirits call,
Their laughter rings, both soft and small.

The moonlight dances on emerald leaves,
Where mystery lingers, and magic breathes.
A tapestry woven from twinkling light,
In these fronds' arms, the world feels right.

With enchantments cradled in nature's hand,
We wander through this marvelous land.
Where vibrant colors burst and twirl,
In the heart of night, we softly swirl.

And as dawn peeks in with golden hue,
We stand enchanted, fresh and new.
With memories spun of joy and grace,
In spirited fronds, we find our place.

Fantasia in the Garden of Echoes

In whispers soft, the echoes play,
In gardens where the dreamers sway.
Vines curl softly, like fingers held,
In fragrant blooms, the heart is swelled.

The sun dips low in velvety skies,
As shadows speak without replies.
A reverie born from petals bright,
In the garden's heart, we take flight.

Each sigh, a story of ages past,
In fluttering wings, the moments cast.
Where laughter lingers, memories blend,
In this sanctuary, time won't end.

Through leafy arches, secrets weave,
In every corner, dreams believe.
With beckoning blooms that seem to glow,
Into the night, our wishes flow.

As moonlight bathes the garden fair,
We sip the magic from the air.
In this fantasia, we'll always roam,
In echoes' arms, we find our home.

Silken Petals on a Mystic Breeze

On silken breeze, the petals float,
In realms where ancient whispers wrote.
A dance of color, soft and free,
In every breath, a mystery.

With butterflies that gently sigh,
While secrets weave and shadows lie.
The fragrant air, a lover's kiss,
In nature's arms, we find our bliss.

As twilight paints the world in gold,
The tales of old begin to unfold.
With every petal that drifts away,
A promise lingers, night shall stay.

In gardens where the fairies dwell,
In stories spun with magic's spell.
We chase the twilight, hearts ablaze,
Through flowing dreams and sunlit haze.

So catch the breeze, let spirits tease,
And tread the path where wonders please.
For in this space, our souls will blend,
On silken petals, time won't end.

Dappled Shadows of a Mythical Realm

In dappled shadows, secrets sigh,
Where whispers dance and moments fly.
Through ancient trees, the stories throng,
In this mythical realm, we belong.

The brook does babble, a gentle tune,
As faeries gather beneath the moon.
With glimmers bright in twilight's fold,
The magic stirs, the brave and bold.

Upon the grass, a tapestry lay,
In colors vibrant, at dusk, at play.
Each step a echo of legends vast,
In dappled shades, we glean the past.

With courage held in heart's embrace,
We wander through this enchanted place.
Where time flows sweetly, a river's dream,
In shadows cast, the world does gleam.

So let us bask in twilight's grace,
As mythical wonders we shall trace.
In the arms of night, our souls ignite,
In dappled shadows, we find our light.

Whispers of Enchanted Arcs

In twilight's hush, the whispers weave,
Of secrets hidden, tales believe.
Owl wings flutter in shadowed flight,
Guiding the lost through the veil of night.

The ancient trees with roots that sigh,
Listened closely, to spirits nigh.
A brook babbles softly in gentle tune,
Beneath the watchful eye of the moon.

Stars twinkle like diamonds in the air,
Each one holding a wish, a prayer.
A breeze carries magic, soft and light,
Embracing the dreamers, hearts ignite.

In the glimmering dusk, dreams take form,
In enchanted arcs, they dance and swarm.
With every heartbeat, promises grow,
In the fabric of night, magic will flow.

So listen close to the tales they spin,
For every ending, a new begins.
In whispers of arcs, may you find,
The magic waiting in heart and mind.

Celestial Spirals in Dreamlight

Beneath the canopies of starlit skies,
The universe twirls, a dance of sighs.
Celestial spirals waltz through the dark,
Painting the night with a shimmering spark.

Moonbeams sprinkle soft on slumbering earth,
Awakening dreams of untold worth.
Floating among clouds, visions untie,
In the embrace of the dawn's first sigh.

Eyes close tightly, as wishes ascend,
Carried by winds, on them we depend.
Through astral pathways where dreams take flight,
Boundless horizons come alive in the night.

Each star a whisper, a story shared,
Of lovers and legends that have dared.
In the depths of slumber, find your way,
To the heavens' embrace, where dreams shall stay.

In celestial spirals, hearts intertwine,
Crafting a destiny ever divine.
So dream, gentle souls, in light's embrace,
For magic and wonder are found in the space.

Rainbows Woven in Velvet Dreams

In velvet realms where shadows drift,
Soft colors blend and gently lift.
Rainbows woven with threads of grace,
Dance on horizons, a timeless place.

Every hue a whispered cheer,
Filling hearts that dare to steer.
Through storms and trials, hope is found,
In the gentle embrace of dreams profound.

Petals bloom under skies so bright,
Carrying whispers of sheer delight.
The laughter of children holds the key,
Unlocking wonders, wild and free.

With every step, the world transforms,
Matching the rhythm of life's warm storms.
In rains that cleanse the weary day,
Vibrant visions dance and play.

So gather your dreams, let colors blend,
For in velvet nights, all stories mend.
In rainbows woven, may you find grace,
A tapestry of dreams, a warm embrace.

Curvaceous Dreams of Starlit Meadows

In meadows where starlit whispers flow,
Curvaceous dreams begin to grow.
Each blade of grass a secret shared,
Within the night, all hearts prepared.

Silvery owls hoot in the twilight's grasp,
As shadows linger, soft and clasp.
Moonlight dances on dew-kissed leaves,
In the stillness, the heart believes.

Gentle winds carry tales of old,
Of adventures grand and spirits bold.
Through meandering paths where the wildflowers sway,
Join the serenade as night greets the day.

Curved horizons in the undulating glow,
Map the dreams that the starlight bestow.
Under vast heavens where wishes take flight,
Hope blooms brightly in the heart of the night.

As slumber caresses, let your soul roam,
In meadows of magic, forever be home.
For in curvaceous dreams, we find our way,
In the embrace of starlit night, we shall stay.